Pearl Loves Her Name

By: Clare McBride

Illustrated By: Stefanie St. Denis

tellwell

Tellwell Talent
www.tellwell.ca

ISBN
978-0-2288-1291-3 (Hardcover)
978-0-2288-1290-6 (Paperback)

In loving memory of Oksana and Quinn, whose thirst for knowledge was unquenchable and whose perspective on life was always joyful. Forever 6 and 4.

"Oh, I hate my name," wailed Pearl.

"Hate your name?" questioned Nanny.

"Yes! All the other girls at school have such elegant names like Elianna or Annabelle or Allegra! My name annoys me!"

"Pearl, your name is very special. Do you know what a pearl is?"

"A pearl is a horribly boring name," declared Pearl.

Nanny tucked Pearl into bed and sat down on the edge of it.

"Have I ever told you the story about my friend Oliver?" asked Nanny.

Pearl shook her head and sighed. She wasn't in the mood for one of Nanny's silly stories.

3

"Well, my friend Oliver lives in the sea, along the coast, on a rocky reef. Oliver is an oyster. He has a grey ridged shell and only one foot."

"Only one foot?" said Pearl.

"Yes, one foot. Aren't you lucky to have two?" Nanny responded.

"One day, Oliver woke up with a horrible pain in his mouth. He went to the mirror and opened wide, but he couldn't see anything. Oliver went downstairs for breakfast and told his mum about his toothache. Much to his surprise, she hurried to the phone to call the dentist. Oliver was so confused by her excitement. He was in pain!"

Pearl imagined what a dentist's office in the sea might look like.

"Getting to the dentist on just one foot takes time. Oliver schlepped along behind his mother, moaning the entire time. She told him to stop his whining and pointed out all the nice scenery. There were schools of anchovies, some lovely barnacles and pretty sea anemones to look at."

"Nanny? What does this silly oyster have to do with my terrible name?" sighed Pearl.

"Patience, Pearl," responded Nanny.

Pearl yawned, leaned down on her elbows and waited for Nanny's next word.

"Ah, yes. Uh huh. I see. Mm hmm," said Dr. Murray, a rather large clam who always seemed to be in a hurry, as he peered into Oliver's mouth.

Dr. Murray stepped back, and Oliver closed his mouth.

"You have your first irritant!" Dr. Murray announced.

"My first what?" asked Oliver.

Oliver's mum beamed from the corner of the room. Oliver still didn't understand her reaction.

"An irritant. Common problem among us molluscs, and there just isn't anything I can do for you. It's a special Oliver problem," rattled off Dr. Murray.

"Nothing?" cried Oliver. "But it hurts!"

"What you need to do, son, is to have patience, and see how it all turns out," said Dr. Murray, spinning the chair around and gesturing for Oliver to get out of it. "Next!"

Oliver felt confused.

"My mouth hurts. The dentist didn't help. I only have one foot. Why me?" he wailed as his mother slogged with him all the way home.

"Now, Oliver, you heard the doctor. There is nothing you can do about this problem other than to have patience. One day at a time, and I bet someday you'll love that you had that little toothache." She winked and gave an all-knowing smile.

"Days and weeks passed," Nanny continued. "As usual, Oliver went to school with his friends, and played with his brothers and sisters on the weekends. His toothache still annoyed him, and Oliver always wondered why the dentist couldn't just pull the irritant out. But he reminded himself to be patient. Oliver soon figured out that by licking the irritant often, the pain lessened a little more each day."

Pearl sat straight up in bed! She didn't like the sound of this irritant being stuck in Oliver's mouth. And this story still had nothing to do with why her name was so awful.

"Nanny," she moaned. "When are you going to get to the part about my name?"

Nanny motioned for her to be quiet and continued with the story.

"One morning as Oliver was eating breakfast, something strange crunched in his mouth. He thought there must've been something in his plankton pancakes! He spit hard, and the thing flew across the table and landed between the salt and pepper shakers."

Pearl rolled her eyes, declaring that was gross.

"Oliver! Manners!" scolded his mum.

"Sorry, Mum." He reached for whatever had been in his mouth. Oliver picked it up. It was a shiny, cream-coloured hard ball. Oliver could see his reflection in it, and it was so smooth.

"Mum! What is this?"

"Ooh, Oliver, it's your pearl! Is your toothache gone?" His mum giggled excitedly.

"Uh, yes. It is," Oliver realized as he ran his tongue around the inside of his mouth.

"But what is a pearl, Mum?"

"Well, Oliver, oysters like us are famous for aches in our mouths. It's so easy to get sand or the like stuck there when you live on an oyster bed. But, like every other oyster out there, you learned to gently tend your ache in your own special Oliver way. And you turned it into something precious - your first pearl!"

"Nanny, eww! I really don't like my name now. Are pearls really an oyster's toothache?" cried Pearl.

"Shh, patience. Listen. Yes, pearls really do exist, and they are made in the mouths of very patient molluscs just like Oliver. And they are beautiful. They're precious gemstones used for making pretty jewellery like my earrings," said Nanny, pointing to the delicate little spheres on her ears.

"Wait a minute, I'm named after a precious gem?" asked Pearl, reaching to feel the smooth finish of one of the pearl earrings.

"Yes, Pearl."

"And these gemstones are made by REAL oysters?"

"Yes, Pearl."

"At the bottom of the sea?" she asked.

"Near the shore, on hard surfaces like big rocks, where all the oysters live together," answered Nanny.

"WOW! That's so cool! I can't wait to tell Allegra! I love my name! If only I had known all along, I'm a precious gem!"

"Yes, you definitely are, Pearl." Nanny smirked as she rose from the bed, tucked Pearl in once more, and kissed her good night.

Pearl smiled. She thought about how Oliver had such a terrible time with his toothache but having patience resulted in his wonderful pearl. She drifted off to sleep, smiling, now knowing the real meaning of her brilliant name.

About the Author

Clare McBride was born in Northern Ireland, the oldest of three girls. At age nine, Clare immigrated with her family to Canada where she spent the rest of her childhood on a prairie grain farm. Since college, Clare has worked in the agricultural industry. She writes to honour the memory of her two daughters, Oksana and Quinn.

Manufactured by Amazon.ca
Bolton, ON

29691771R00017